God created the first man, Adam, and the first woman, Eve. They lived in the Garden of Eden. Find all the differences you can between these two pictures of Eden.
You will find the story of Adam and Eve in Genesis 2:7–25.

The artist has made lots of deliberate mistakes in this picture of Adam and Eve in the Garden of Eden.
Can you find them all?
Find the story of Adam and Eve in Genesis 2:7–25. What clothes did they wear?

Find out what's happening in this picture of the Garden of Eden.
Join up the numbered dots. What is about to trick Eve into disobeying God?
You can find this story in Genesis 3:1–7.

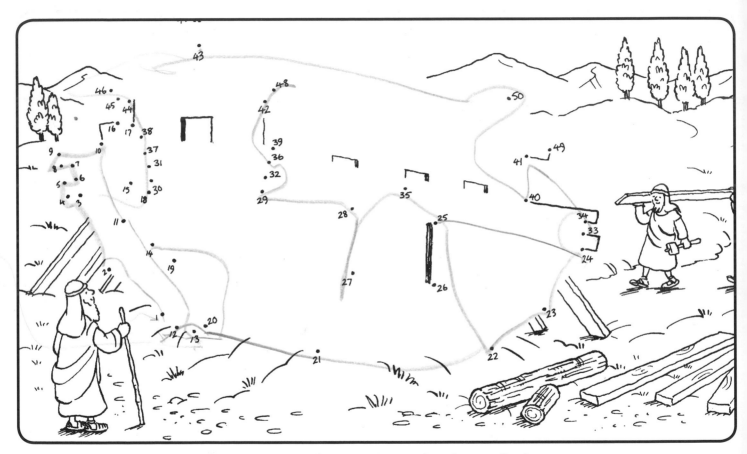

What's going on here? Join up the dots to find out.
What is old Noah building? Why? But there's no water in sight.
You can find this story in Genesis 6:9–22.

Find ten differences between these two pictures of Noah and his family building the ark.
Why did Noah build his ark?
Read Genesis 6:9–22. What happened next?

Can you find all the funny mistakes the artist has made
in this picture of the ark during the great flood?
You can read this story in Genesis chapters 6–9. How many mistakes did you find?

Everyone is now safe aboard the ark.
Can you find all the deliberate funny mistakes in this picture?
Read Genesis 7:13–20. Who went into the ark?

Noah, his family, and the animals were safe in the ark for forty days during the great flood.
Can you find ten upside-down raindrops in this picture?
Look up the story of Noah and the great flood in Genesis 6:9–8:22.

Noah can see dry land.
Find the way for the ark to get to the dry land without crossing any lines.
Read Genesis chapters 7 and 8. How did Noah find out there was dry land?

Here are six pictures telling the story of Noah and the great flood – but they're all mixed up.
Number them in the right order.
You can read the whole story in Genesis 6:1 – 9:17.

Jacob tricked his father by pretending to be his twin brother, Esau.
He put goats' skin on his arms to pretend he was hairy, like his brother.
Can you find Esau hiding in this picture? *Read Genesis 27:1–35.*

Jacob ran away from his brother Esau. He escaped to the desert and slept outdoors.
Now join up the dots. Jacob dreamed of a ladder going up to heaven.
How many a_ _ _ _ _ are on the ladder? *You can find this story in Genesis 28:10–22.*

Jacob slept in the desert, where he had an amazing dream.
Can you find all the deliberate mistakes the artist has put into this picture?
Read this story in Genesis 28:10–22. How many mistakes did you discover?

13

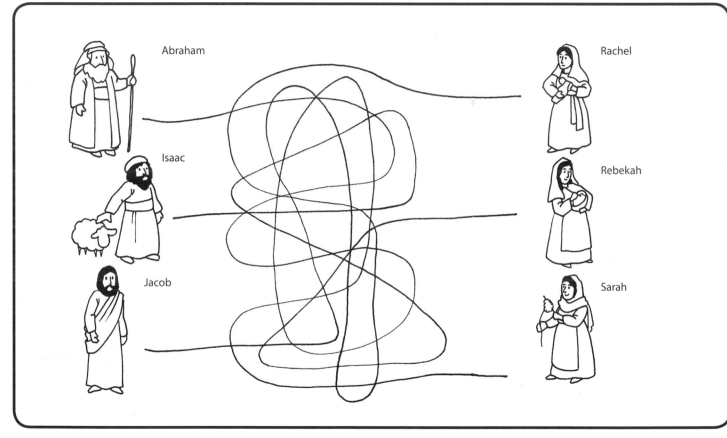

Here are Abraham, his son Isaac, and his grandson Jacob.
Follow the lines to link them with their wives.
Find some clues in Genesis 17:19, 25:20 and 29:22.

Jacob had a big family, but loved his son Joseph more than all his other boys.
What is Joseph wearing here? Join the dots to find out.
Read the whole story in Genesis 37:3-4.

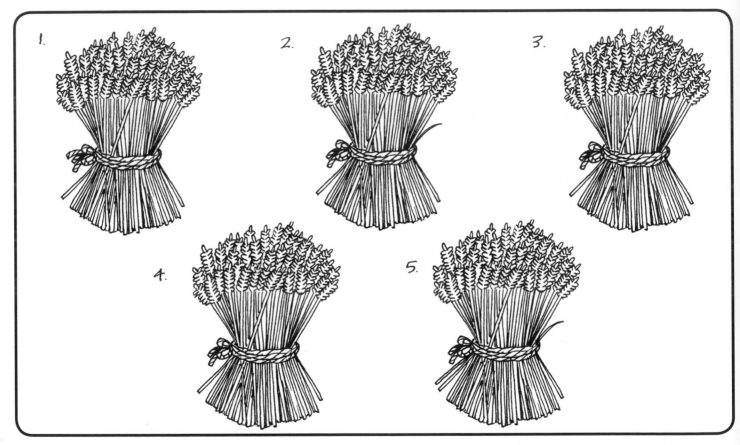

Joseph told his brothers that, in his dream, their sheaves of grain bowed down to his sheaf. Which two sheaves of grain are exactly the same? Why were Joseph's brothers angry?
Read this story in Genesis 37:5–8.

What is happening here? Join up the dots to find out.
Who was sold by his brothers for twenty pieces of silver?
You can find this story in Genesis 37:19–36.

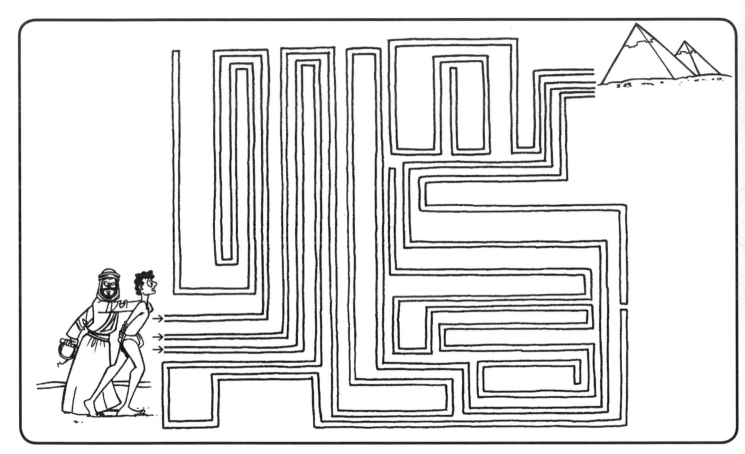

Traders took Joseph across the desert to become a slave in Egypt.
Can you help them find the road that leads to the pyramids of Egypt?
Read this story in Genesis 37:12–28.

In Egypt Joseph worked for an army captain called Potiphar.
Potiphar's wife tried to make Joseph do something wrong. *Read Genesis 39:1–5.*
Can you find all the funny mistakes in this picture of Joseph with Potiphar's wife?

Potiphar sent Joseph to prison. In prison, Pharaoh's baker and butler had strange dreams. Joseph explained what their dreams meant. Which is the baker and which is the butler here? Follow the paths to find out. *You can read this story in your Bible. Read Genesis 40:1–23.*

Joseph is explaining the extraordinary dreams of Pharaoh, king of Egypt.
Write what Joseph is saying in the speech bubble.
Read Genesis 41:15–32 to help you.

Pharaoh, king of Egypt, freed Joseph from prison and put him in charge of storing grain. Join up the dots to find out what's happening.
Read this story in Genesis 41:41–57. For how many years were there good harvests?

When their food ran out, Joseph's brothers came to Egypt to buy grain.
They took sacks of grain back home.
Which two sacks are exactly the same? *Read Genesis chapter 42.*

Finally, Jacob and all his sons came to live in Egypt.
Joseph is greeting his father and brothers when they arrive.
How many crazy mistakes can you find here? *Read this story in Genesis 46:1 – 47:12.*

The artist has drawn pictures of different adventures in Joseph's life. But he muddled them up.
Can you number them in the right order?
Look in Genesis 37–45 to help you.

Moses' mother hid her baby son to prevent Pharaoh's soldiers from killing him.
Where did Pharaoh's daughter find baby Moses?
Join up the numbered dots to find the answer. *You can read this story in Exodus 2:1–10.*

When he grew up, Moses saw a bush burning in the desert one day.
Find ten differences between the two pictures.
You can read what happened in Exodus 3:1–14. What was odd about the burning bush?

Later Moses helped his people escape from Egypt. He led his people through the Red Sea.
The artist has included lots of deliberate mistakes. How many can you see?
Read this story in Exodus chapter 14.

Moses climbed Mount Sinai to receive special laws from God. He's holding two stones with the Ten Commandments on them. There are ten differences between the two pictures: can you find them all? *Read this story in Exodus 19:16–19 and 24:12–13.*

Joshua took his army of Israelites to the city of Jericho.
Join up the dots. After the soldiers marched around the city for seven days, the trumpets sounded.
Then what happened? *You can find this story in Joshua 6:1–20.*

The giant Goliath challenged the Israelites to fight him.
Fill in his speech bubble. *Read 1 Samuel 17:8–11 to help you.*
Now finish the picture with felt-tips or crayons. Who offered to fight Goliath?

Here is David hurling a sling-stone at the giant Goliath.
The artist has made at least ten deliberate mistakes. Can you find all of them?
Read this story in 1 Samuel 17:48–51.

Here are six pictures from the story of David – but they're muddled up.
Number them in the right order.
Look at 1 Samuel 16–17 and 2 Samuel 5–6 to help you. What instrument is David playing?

While the prophet Elijah was hiding in the desert, God sent ravens to feed him. Join up the dots to complete the picture – then finish it with felt-tips or crayons. *Read this story in 1 Kings 17:1–6.* What food did the birds bring Elijah?

Elijah built a stone altar. Then he prayed to God to send fire on it.
Join up the dots. Can you see what happened next?
You can find this story in 1 Kings 18:18–39.

When Elijah grew old, God chose Elisha to take over his work.
Elijah was parted from the prophet Elisha in a strange way.
Join up the dots to find out how. *Read this story in 2 Kings 2:6–14.*

Naaman had a terrible skin disease. His servant told Naaman that God's prophet Elisha might be able to cure him. Here she is telling Naaman where to go to be healed.
Write what she is saying in her speech bubble. *Read 2 Kings 5:2–5 to help you.*

Naaman is dipping in the River Jordan, as the prophet Elisha told him to.
Join up the dots to complete the picture.
How many times did Naaman dip before he was clean? *Read 2 Kings 5:8–14 to find out.*

Here are six pictures from the story of Daniel – but they're in the wrong order.
Number them in the right order.
Look at Daniel 5–6 to help you. What is Daniel pointing to on the wall?

God told Jonah to go and preach in Nineveh. What did Jonah do?
Read Jonah 1:1–3 to find out.
Can you find all the crazy mistakes here?

Jonah disobeyed God.
Sailors threw him into the sea during a terrible storm.
Join up the dots to complete the picture. *You can read about this in Jonah 1:3–16.*

Jonah spent three days inside a great fish.
Can you show him how to get to shore again?
You can read this part of the story of Jonah in Jonah 1:1–17.

After three days the great fish spat out Jonah onto the seashore.
What is Jonah saying here? Fill in his speech bubble.
Read Jonah 2:1–10 to help you.

Baby Jesus was born in Bethlehem. Shepherds rushed to the stable to find the newborn baby.
They told Mary an angel had told them where to go.
Join up the dots to complete the picture. *Read the whole story in Luke 2:8–20.*

When he grew up, Jesus called twelve men to be his special friends, the disciples.
Can you find all the differences between these two pictures?
Read the story in Luke 6:12–16.

One night a man called Nicodemus visited Jesus secretly.
Find all the funny mistakes in the picture.
Read what Nicodemus and Jesus talked about in John 3:1–15.

One day four friends carried a sick man to see Jesus.
Join up the dots. What is happening here?
Read Luke 5:17–19 to get the whole story.

Four friends are lowering the sick man down to Jesus.
How many funny mistakes can you find in this picture?
Read this story in Luke 5:17–19.

One day Jesus was visiting the city of Jericho.
A very small man named Zacchaeus wanted to see Jesus.
Join up the dots to find out how he did this. *Read this story in Luke 19:1–10.*

Zacchaeus was so small that he had to climb a tree to see Jesus.
Can you find ten differences between these two pictures of Jesus talking to Zacchaeus in the tree?
Read Luke 19:1–10 for the whole story. What happened next?

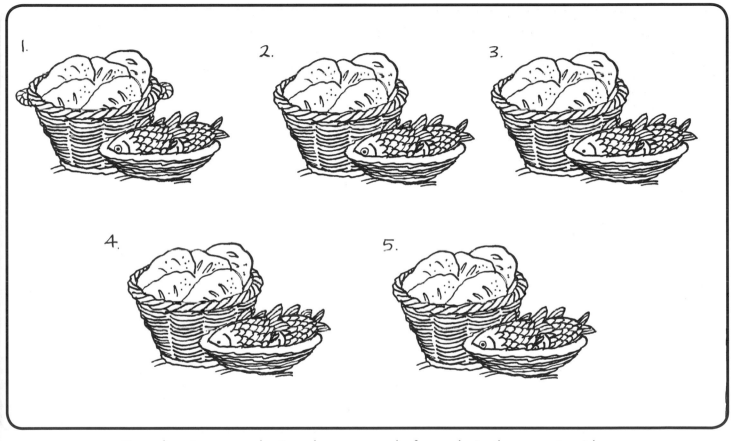

One day Jesus spoke to a huge crowd of people in the countryside.
They were all hungry, but only one boy had food. *Read this story in John 6:5–15.*
Here are five drawings of the boy's lunch of loaves and fishes. Which two are exactly the same?

Jesus broke the bread the boy gave him before he gave it to the crowd.
Copy this picture into the blank box. Now finish it with your crayons or felt-tips.
Read John 6:11 to find out what Jesus did before he broke the bread.

Here are six different pictures of Jesus feeding the crowd of people.
Can you put them in the right order? *Read this story again in John 6:5–15.*
Number the pictures 1–6, then fill them in with your crayons or felt-tips.

This shepherd has lost one of his 100 sheep. Help him find the lost sheep.
Which is the right way through the maze?
Read Jesus' story of the lost sheep in Luke 15:1–7.

Jesus told a story about a man who set out to walk from Jerusalem to Jericho.
On the road, thieves attacked the man. Join up the dots.
Read Luke 10:30. Who is running off?

The man lay injured on the road. A priest came past, but didn't help.
Can you find all ten silly mistakes here?
Read this story in Luke 10:30–36.

At last a kind, good stranger came past. He looked after the man who had been robbed.
Find ten little differences between the two pictures.
You can read this story in Luke 10:25–37.

The man who helped the injured man is often called the "good Samaritan".
Where is he taking the man who had been hurt?
Join the numbered dots to find out. *Read Luke 10:34.*

Here are six scenes from the story of the good Samaritan. They are all muddled up.
Can you number them in the right order?
Read the whole story in Luke 10:30–37.

Jesus told a story about two house-builders.
This house is built on rock. It will stand firm in the storm.
Draw in lightning and rain. *Read Luke 6:46–48.*

Here are the two houses, one built by a wise man, the other by a foolish man.
Which is which? Can you find ten differences between the two pictures?
Read this story in Matthew 7:24–27.

Jesus told a story about a father who had two sons. The younger son decided to leave home. The artist has drawn the father saying goodbye, but forgot to draw the boy leaving. Add the younger son and finish the picture. *Read this story in Luke 15:11–13.*

Jesus spoke to Saul when he was on his way to Damascus. Saul was blinded.
Can you find eight plants hidden in the picture?
Read the story in Acts 9:1–19. Saul continued his journey to Damascus, where he was healed.

Saul became a Christian and later changed his name to Paul. He was in great danger.
Read the whole story in Acts 9:19b–30. Can you help Saul escape from Damascus?
Find the way through the maze without crossing any lines.